Clayton Jr

temporama

NOBROW PRESS
London

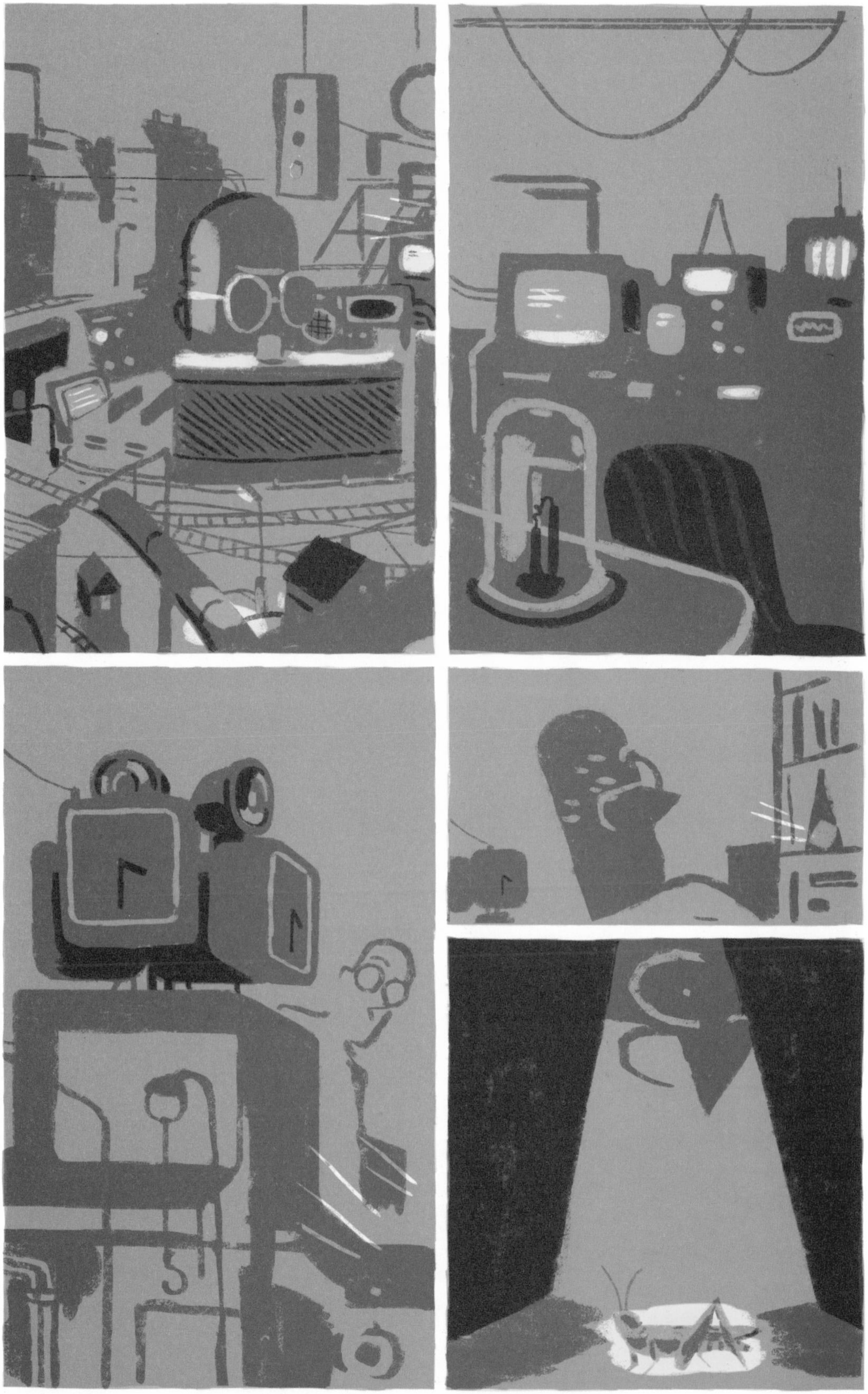

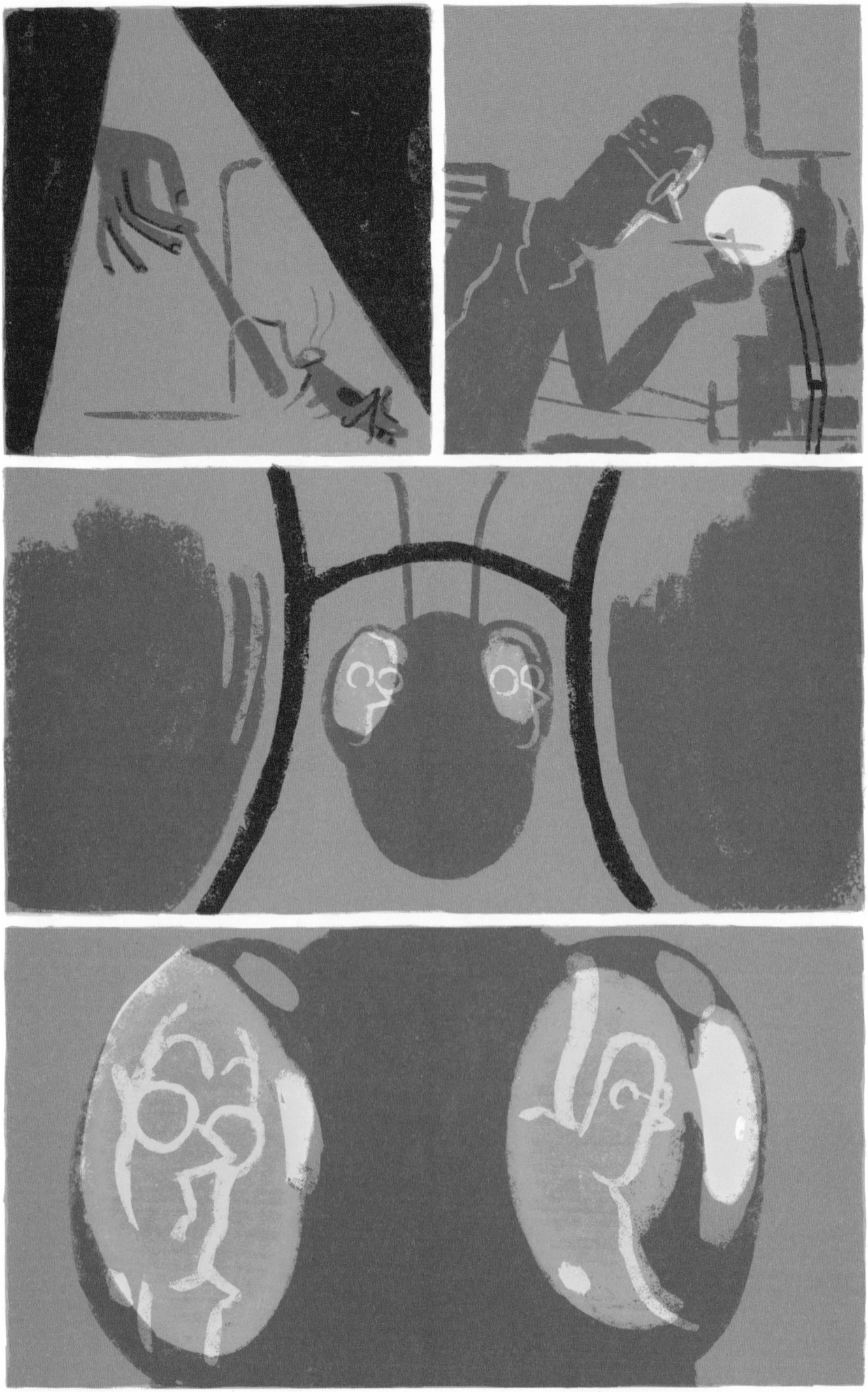

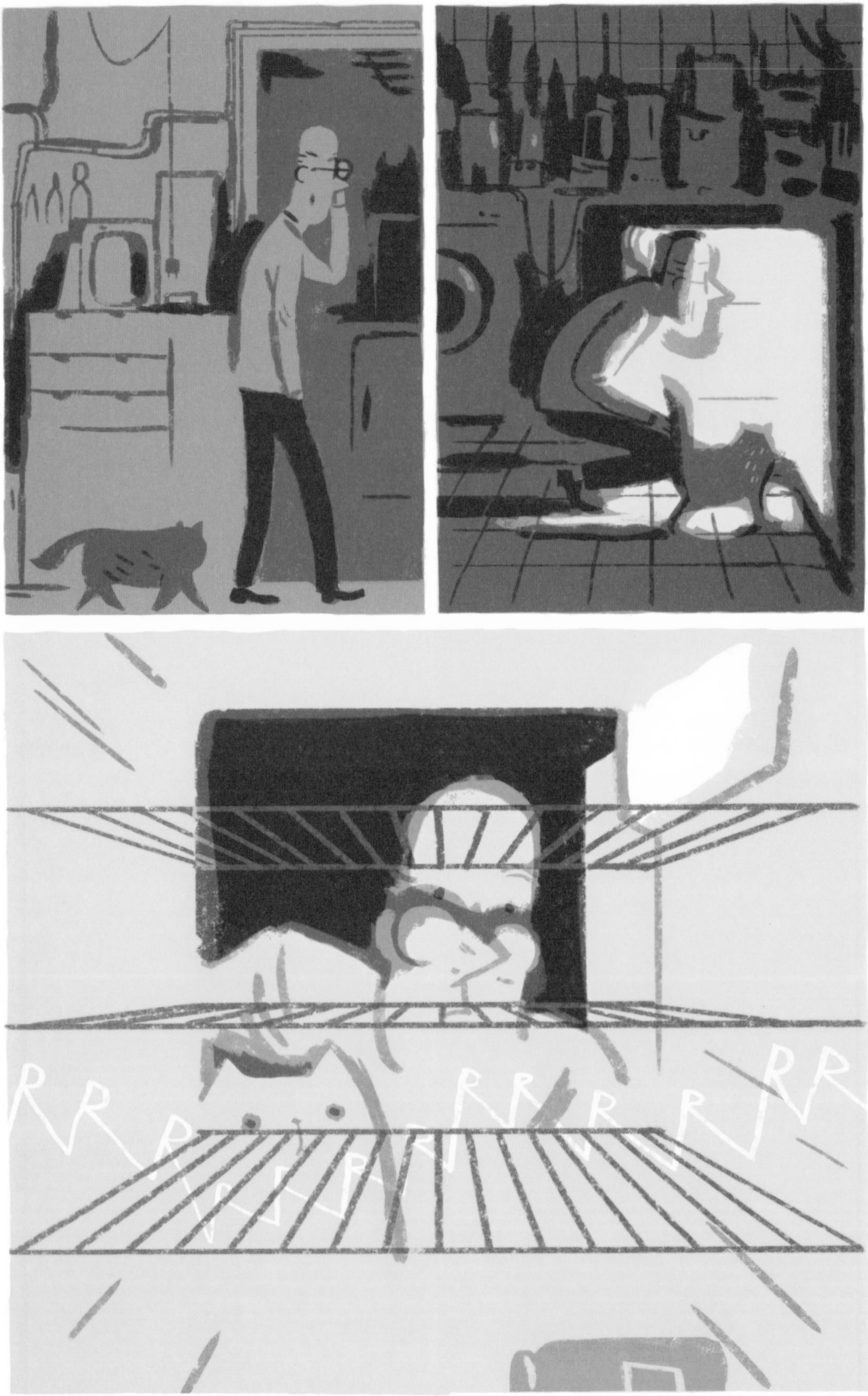

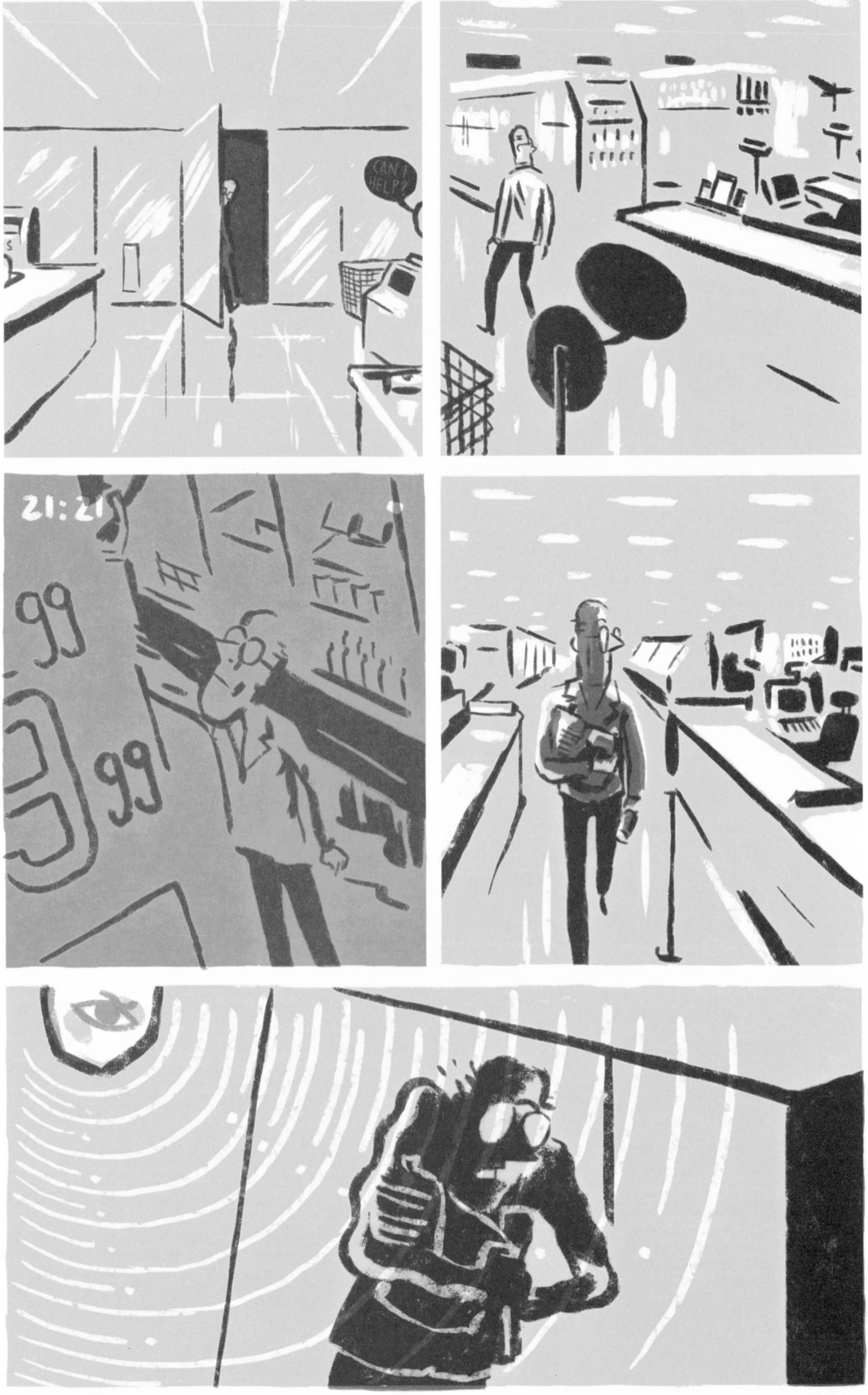
CAN I HELP?
21:21
99
99

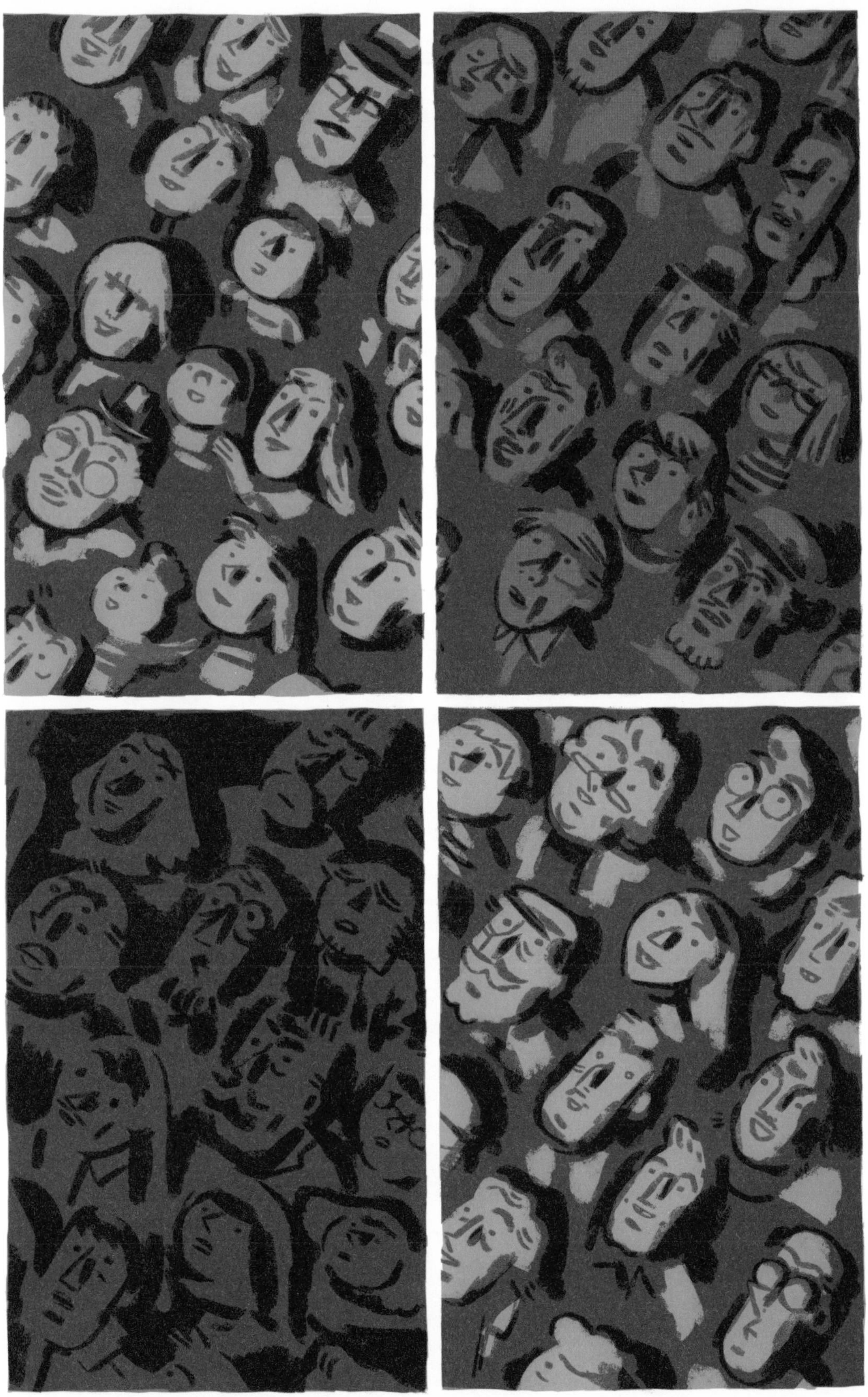

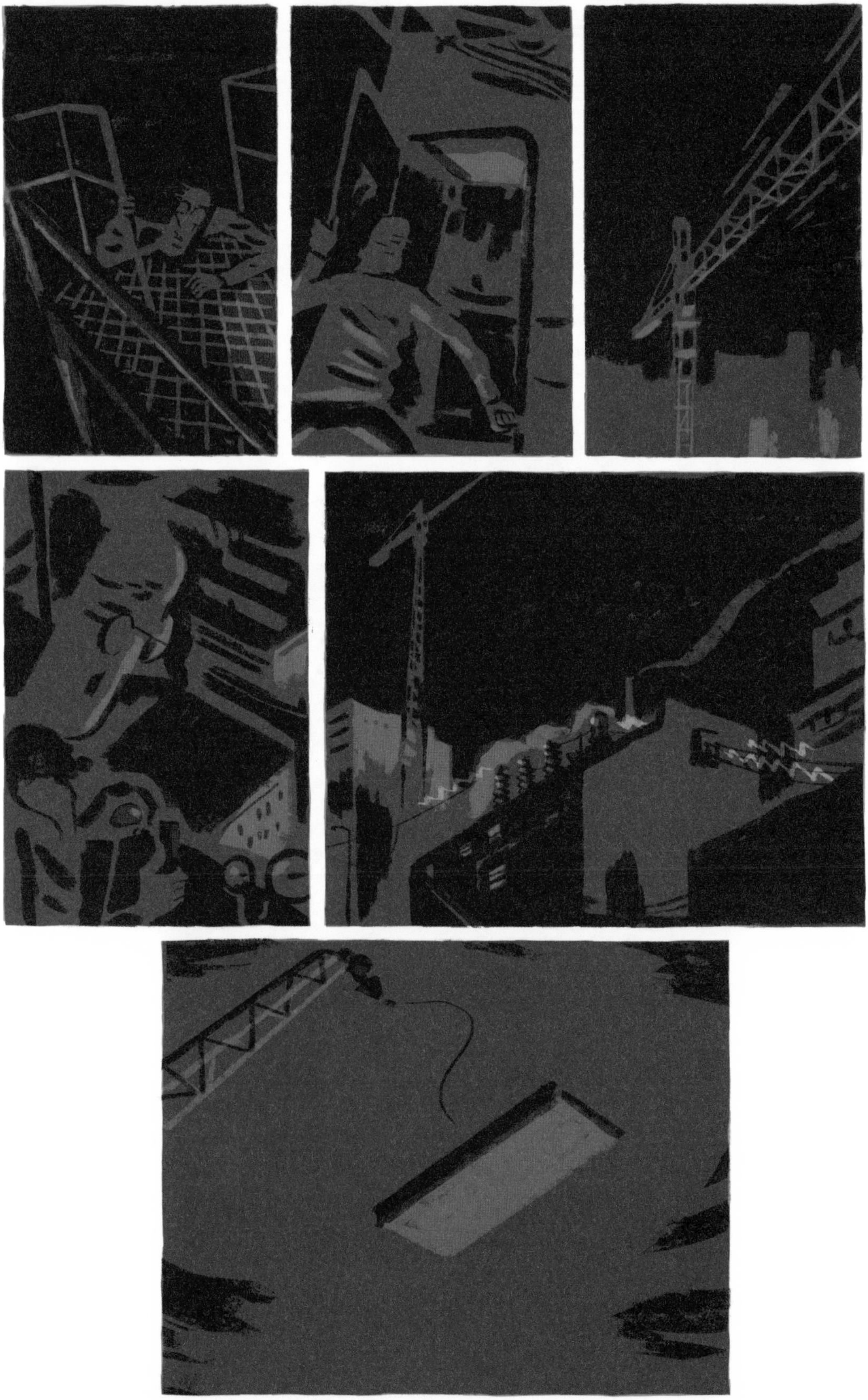